W9-BZA-712

Withdrawn

LONG-ARMED LUDY

and the First Women's Olympics

Based on the True Story of Lucile Ellerbe Godbold

Jean L. S. Patrick
Illustrated by Adam Gustavson

ini Charlesbridge

No one really knows how Ludy's arms got so long.

Maybe too much
tug-o'-warrin'
with the dogs . . .

"Look out below!"

Maybe too much haulin'
water to the hogs . . .

Or maybe too much swingin'
from the tree branches with
all her sisters and brothers
hangin' on.

Come to think of it,
maybe that's what made
Ludy's arms so *strong*.

When Ludy set off for Winthrop College in 1917, she was six feet tall and skinnier than a Carolina pine. In fact, if she turned sideways, you'd think she had disappeared.

But you could always spot Ludy on the athletic field . . .

Sprintin' . . .

Scorin' . . .

Cheerin' . . .

Supportin' . . .

In every sport, Ludy used her long arms to encourage her teammates.

"You can do it!"

During her final year on the track team, Ludy tried the shot put. "Give it a ride," urged Coach Bartlett.

Ludy scooped up the heavy iron ball and placed it between her fingers. She bent her knees, *pushed* her long arm upward, and released! The ball soared across the sky.

"Her throw was almost as long as three automobiles!"

"Thunderin' cannonballs!"

"Unbelievable!"

Her heart boomed. Her long arm tingled. She loved the explosion of power.

So Ludy trained to become a shot-putter. Every muscle needed to be strong.

She lifted dumbbells 'til her arms turned to noodles. She ran 'til her toes cried for mercy. And she did so many leg squats that her feet disappeared in the dust.

She wanted to become a champion.

All that liftin' and runnin' and squattin' paid off. At a Winthrop College track meet in the spring of 1922, Ludy surprised everyone. She set an American record in the shot put with a throw of 35 feet, 6 ¼ inches.

And before you could say "Carolina cannonball," Ludy and Coach Bartlett hopped on a train. They headed north to an important track meet in New York.

There, the best athletes would try out for an international meet called the Women's Olympics.

When they arrived at the tryout meet, more than a hundred women were runnin' and jumpin' and throwin'. Ludy eyed the muscular shot-putters. Did she even have a chance?

"Give it a ride," urged Coach Bartlett.

Ludy placed the iron ball between her fingers. She focused. Pushed! Released!

The officials measured. The announcer boomed. "35 feet, 11 inches! Miss Lucile Godbold has set a new American record!"

Coach Bartlett flung her clipboard into the clouds.

"You won!" she cried. "You're headed to the Women's Olympics in Paris, France!"

Ludy whooped, "Ooh la la!"

"Cloud bustin' cantaloupes!"

"She broke her own record!"

But Ludy's smile soon sagged.

"I'd love to go to the Women's Olympics," she told Coach Bartlett. "I'd be honored right down to the tips of my toes. But I just don't have the money."

The train ride back to South Carolina was quiet.

When they arrived at Winthrop College, nearly thirteen hundred women welcomed Ludy home, cheerin' and stompin' 'til the floor sprouted splinters.

Ludy was stunned. She couldn't bear to tell them the bad news. So she pushed out a smile . . . and kept on training.

More liftin', more runnin'. More squattin', more puttin'.
Sweat dribbled down Ludy's ankles and into her old shoes.
More than anything she wanted to go to the Women's Olympics.
But how would she come up with the money? It would be impossible.
Ludy cradled the iron ball in her hands. It felt as heavy as the
world. Maybe even heavier. But Ludy hung on.

One morning Ludy ran past President Johnson's office. He opened the door and whooshed her inside.

"Good news!" he said. "Winthrop's thirteen hundred students and teachers are donating money so you can go to France."

Ludy's skinny backside nearly slipped off the chair. She'd be going to the Women's Olympics!

"I promise to win," she vowed. "Not just for myself, but for everyone helping me."

For the next two months, Ludy trained twice as hard. At the Women's Olympics, she'd have to throw with *both* of her long arms. First with her right, then with her left.

"Go, Ludy!"

On August 1, Ludy climbed the gangplank of the *Aquitania* for the six-day voyage to France.

She shook hands with her new coach, Dr. Stewart. Would he be strict?

She smiled at her new teammates. Would they be kind?

The ship began to rock and sway. *Blubberin' codfish!* She'd have to train on board.

More liftin', more runnin'. More squattin', more puttin'.

Ludy only fed one to the fish.

When Ludy and her new friends reached Paris . . . *Ooh la la!*
Every morning they practiced for two hours. But in the
afternoons and evenings, they opened their eyes to the world.
The battlefields . . . Versailles . . . the Louvre.

The pastry shops smelled like heaven, but Dr. Stewart only
allowed them to drool.

The night before the Women's Olympics, Ludy lay awake in bed.
The moon, round and shiny, stared through her window.
Ludy stared back. Was she good enough to win?

On the morning of August 20, 1922, Ludy entered Pershing Stadium for the Women's Olympics. Twenty thousand fans roared from the stands.

Ludy's teammates handed her Old Glory. When the wind tugged, she gripped the flag tighter. When the Americans cheered, she lifted it higher.

That afternoon Ludy faced the best women shot-putters in the world. She knew the hardest fight would come from France's world-record holder, Violette Gouraud-Morris.

Violette stepped into the circle and pawed the ground with her toe. She heaved with her right arm. She heaved with her left arm. The two throws were added together. Total distance . . . 65 feet, 1 ½ inches!

"Gulp."

Ludy's long arms wobbled like French custard. How could she beat that throw?

Then she heard Dr. Stewart holler, "Now, Ludy! You show 'em what you can do!"

Ludy thought of Coach Bartlett and her thirteen hundred friends at college. She thought of her family back home.

"Give it a ride," she whispered to herself.

She placed the iron ball between the fingers of her right hand. She focused. Pushed! Released!

She placed the iron ball between the fingers of her left hand. She focused. Pushed! Released!

"Total distance . . . 66 feet, 4 ⅛ inches!" cried the official. "Miss Lucile Godbold of the United States is the winner!"

The American flag shot up the pole. The band blasted *The Star-Spangled Banner* . . . twice!

Ludy's heart swelled. Tears leaped from her cheekbones and bounced off the curve of her smile. She had set a new world record.

That evening Ludy and her new friends received their medals.

After the banquet they ate so much French pastry, they nearly popped!

Ludy wanted to wrap her long, strong arms around every person who had helped her compete at the Women's Olympics.

Thanks to the big hearts of so many, she had become a champion.

More About Ludy

Lucile (Ludy) Godbold was born in Marion County, South Carolina, on May 31, 1900. She attended Winthrop College, a women's college in Rock Hill, South Carolina, where she excelled in field hockey, basketball, and track.

Ludy was one of fifteen athletes originally selected for the United States Women's Olympic team. After winning the eight-pound shot put, she placed third in the javelin (throwing with each arm!), third in the 1000-meter run, and fourth in the 300-meter run. In the exhibition events, she won the triple jump and placed second in the basketball throw.

After the Women's Olympics, Ludy taught physical education for fifty-eight years at Columbia College in Columbia, South Carolina. She died on April 5, 1981.

Ludy, age 22, at the Women's Olympics. (Image courtesy of the Louise Pettus Archives at Winthrop University.)

The Women's Olympics

For years women were not allowed to compete in track and field events at the Olympics. Frustrated, Alice Milliat of France organized an international track meet called "The Women's Olympics."

On August 20, 1922, seventy-seven women from France, Great Britain, Switzerland, Czechoslovakia, and the United States competed in eleven official events and four exhibition events at Pershing Stadium in Paris, France.

The International Olympic Committee demanded that the meet not use the word "Olympics." However, women continued to compete in 1926, 1930, and 1934 in the renamed "Women's World Games."

The modern Olympics began to include women's track and field events in 1928, but with only five events. The shot put was not included until 1948—twenty-six years after Ludy won at the first Women's Olympics.

Currently, women compete in twenty-three Olympic track and field events.

Ludy on the far left, aboard the *Aquitania*, en route to France with the majority of the United States Women's Olympic team, August 1922. (Photo courtesy of the Lucile Godbold Papers, J. Drake Edens Library Archives, Columbia College, Columbia, S.C.)

Author's Note

I first discovered Ludy's story when I ran across a rollicking speech she gave to the Winthrop students after the Women's Olympics. I laughed out loud as she described her training, the competition, and the fun she had at the international banquet following the meet.

But Ludy didn't become fully alive to me until I traveled to South Carolina to research her story. With awe, I read Ludy's diary, paged through her scrapbook, and saw her small, precious medals. Every item brimmed with emotion and determination.

Most thrilling was finding the auditorium where Ludy looked upon the Winthrop student body. As I stood on the stage, I realized her story wasn't just about sports, but about people helping people.

I'd like to thank everyone who helped me, including the librarians and archivists at Winthrop University and Columbia College, the individuals who shared memories of "Miss Ludy's" heart and humor, and Alexandra Penfold, Julie Bliven, and especially Bonnie Christensen, who first encouraged me to share Ludy's story.

Selected bibliography

"Jeux Olympiques Féminins." Programme Officiel. 20 Août 1922.

"'Our Ludy' Comes Home." Winthrop College News 10, no. 5. (October 20, 1922).

Tricard, Louise Mead. *American Women's Track and Field: A History, 1895 through 1980*. Jefferson, NC: McFarland & Co., 1996.

In memory of Bonnie Christensen—J. L. S. P.

For Gianna, DJ, and Mia—A. G.

Text copyright © 2017 by Jean L. S. Patrick
Illustrations copyright © 2017 Adam Gustavson
All rights reserved, including the right of reproduction in whole or in part in any form.
Charlesbridge and colophon are registered trademarks of Charlesbridge Publishing, Inc.

Published by Charlesbridge
85 Main Street
Watertown, MA 02472
(617) 926-0329
www.charlesbridge.com

Library of Congress Cataloging-in-Publication Data
Names: Patrick, Jean L. S.
Title: Long-armed Ludy and the first women's Olympics : based on the true story of Lucile Ellerbe Godbold / Jean L. S. Patrick ; illustrated by Adam Gustavson.
Description: Watertown, MA : Charlesbridge, [2017]
Identifiers: LCCN 2015043920 (print) | LCCN 2016026196 (ebook) | ISBN 9781580895460 (reinforced for library use) | ISBN 9781632895776 (ebook) | ISBN 9781632895783 (ebook pdf)
Subjects: LCSH: Godbold, Lucile, 1900–1981—Juvenile literature. | Track and field athletes—United States—Biography—Juvenile literature. | Women track and field athletes—United States—Biography—Juvenile literature. | Olympics—Juvenile literature.
Classification: LCC GV697.G54 P38 2017 (print) | LCC GV697.G54 (ebook) | DDC 796.42092 [B] —dc23
LC record available at https://lccn.loc.gov/2015043920

Printed in China
(hc) 10 9 8 7 6 5 4 3 2 1

The full page illustrations were executed in oil paint on prepared paper; the spot illustrations were completed using gouache on watercolor paper
Display type hand-lettered by Adam Gustavson
Text type set in Arno Pro by Adobe Systems
Color separations by Colourscan Print Co Pte Ltd, Singapore
Printed by 1010 Printing International Limited in Huizhou, Guangdong, China
Production supervision by Brian G. Walker
Designed by Martha MacLeod Sikkema